As you journey back to  n
moving and living a ful! h
    this journaling experience you ....
RELEASE THE HURTS and live a life of Purpose and Power!

"Let go of the past and open the door to your Future"

Audrey Brooks

Release the Hurt Affirmation Journal
Affirmations to help you move past the hurts of Yesterday

Releasing the past helps me to redirect
my mind, recreate my purpose,
and restore my heart;
(Psalms 51:10)

The thoughts of the past are no longer
holding me captive
(John 8:32)

I choose to love and forgive myself
(Proverbs 19:8)

I will no longer focus on the hurts of
yesterday but work to live
a purpose driven life.
(Philippians 3:13-14)

The victor in me can no longer
live as a victim
(victim 2 victor)
(1 Corinthians 15:57)

My positive attitude will lead me to
positive outcomes
(Romans 12:2)

My past does not determine who I am but
has prepared me for who I am to become
(Psalm 139:13-15)

The recollection of my past has made me
wiser and stronger
(Isaiah 43:18-19)

I have the power to choose who or what
I become
(Isaiah 40:29)

I broke up with my past to have a
relationship with my future
(John 8:36)

I am liberated from the things of the past
(Romans 8:1-2)

Only good thoughts shall inhabit my mind
(2 Timothy 1:7)

I am purposed for Greatness and
I shall dwell in it
(1 Peter 2:9)

I welcome forgiveness, peace, trust,
acceptance and love in my life
(Colossians 3:12-14)

I am releasing any hurts from my past and moving forward
(2 Corinthians 5:17)

I see goodness in each day and I
rejoice in it
(Psalm 118:24)

I have the power to speak and see those
things before they exist
(Romans 4:17)

_____

_____

_____

_____

_____

_____

_____

_____

_____

_____

_____

_____

_____

I release my past without regrets, I embrace my today with confidence and I move in my future without fear.
(2 Timothy 1:7)

_____
_____
_____
_____
_____
_____
_____
_____
_____
_____
_____
_____
_____
_____

I must speak life into my life daily
(Proverbs 4:23)

_____

_____

_____

_____

_____

_____

_____

_____

_____

_____

_____

_____

_____

_____

A new mindset reaps new results
(2 Corinthians 10:5)

I have the strength to grow through what I went through
(Philippians 4:13)

I choose to focus on what I have today rather than what I lost in the past
(Hebrews 13:5)

My past experiences cannot hinder my
future experiences
(2 Timothy 3:15)

_____

_____

_____

_____

_____

_____

_____

_____

_____

_____

_____

_____

_____

_____

My past chapters are only a prelude to
my story.
(Psalm 66:16)

My present emotions will no longer keep
my past alive
(1 Peter 5:10)

I choose to heal the past and
release my future
(John 14:27)

I will no longer dance to the music
of my past
(Psalm 37:1-6)

The more I am thankful for life, the more life gives me to be thankful for
(Jeremiah 30:19)

I shall exhale the things of my past and
inhale the things of today
(Job 33:4)

My happiness is experienced
one day at a time
(Philippians 4:6)

I have released the weight of the past and
I now walk in freedom
(Matthew 11:28)

My past snapshots are not permanent
pictures of my future
(2 Corinthians 4:16-18)

What you celebrate expands
(Psalms 98:4)

I give myself permission to
live laugh and love
(Psalms 126:2-3)

Faith, trust, and time have replaced the hurt and pain with purpose and freedom
(Romans 15:13)

I will focus on what's important, no longer
wasting the limitless entities of time and
energy on things of the past.
(Ephesians 5:15-16)

The success in my future is limitless
(Psalm 147:5)

Life is too short to dwell on the negativity,
I choose to radiate in love, joy, and gratitude
(Philippians 4:8)

I am free to create my own reality; nothing stands between me and my highest good.
(Matthew 21:22)

I release the chains of the past and I take
control of my destiny
(Jeremiah 40:4)

_____

_____

_____

_____

_____

_____

_____

_____

_____

_____

_____

_____

_____

I release the need to impress others and
I choose to accept who I am
(Genesis 1:27)

I stand boldly in my power and honor all
that is important to me
(Luke 21:19)

Each day is full of endless
possibilities and opportunities
(Psalms 84:11)

As CEO of my life I manage the outcomes
(James 2:26)

Each day I strive to be better than
the day before
(Ephesians 2:10)

I have the power to reshape my thoughts and
release the hurts of the past
(2 Timothy 1:7)

_____

_____

_____

_____

_____

_____

_____

_____

_____

_____

_____

_____

_____

_____

I have the power to accomplish my
dreams and visions
(Habakkuk 2:2)

_____

_____

_____

_____

_____

_____

_____

_____

_____

_____

_____

_____

_____

Each day I am becoming more of who I
was created to be
(Exodus 9:16)

Everything I need is in me to create
the success I want
(Philippians 4:13)

I am free, fierce, and fearless
(2 Corinthians 3:17)

I relinquish my past for it serves no
purpose in my present
(Job 17:9)

_____

_____

_____

_____

_____

_____

_____

_____

_____

_____

_____

_____

_____

_____

_____

I am grounded with self-love, self-esteem, self-reliance, self-determination, and self-appreciation
(Proverbs 31:25)

Confident, courage, and content
flow through me
(Ephesians 6:10)

I am thankful for each lesson
my past taught me
(Isaiah 43:18-19)

_____
_____
_____
_____
_____
_____
_____
_____
_____
_____
_____
_____
_____
_____
_____

I forgive my past and I
release myself from it
(Colossians 3:13)

I am healed, delivered, and set free
from the things of my past
(Romans 8:28-29)

My past will not control nor distract me
from living in my present
(Galatians 2:20-22)

_____
_____
_____
_____
_____
_____
_____
_____
_____
_____
_____
_____
_____
_____
_____
_____